I DECLARE

Personal Application Guide

Also by Joel Osteen

I Declare

Every Day a Friday

Every Day a Friday Journal

Daily Readings from Every Day a Friday

Your Best Life Now

Daily Readings from Your Best Life Now

Starting Your Best Life Now

Your Best Life Now Study Guide

Your Best Life Now for Moms

Your Best Life Begins Each Morning

Your Best Life Now Journal

Available from FaithWords wherever books are sold.

I DECLARE

Personal Application Guide

JOEL OSTEEN

New York • Boston • Nashville

Unless otherwise indicated, Scriptures are taken from the *Holy Bible*, New International Version® NIV®. Copyright © 1973, 1978, 1984, 2011 by Biblica, Inc.™ Used by permission. All rights reserved worldwide.

Scripture quotations noted AMP are from the *Amplified Bible*. Copyright © 1954, 1958, 1962, 1964, 1965, 1987 by The Lockman Foundation. All rights reserved. Used by permission. (www.Lockman.org)

Scriptures noted NLT are taken from the *Holy Bible*, New Living Translation, copyright © 1996, 2004, 2007 by Tyndale House Foundation. Used by permission of Tyndale House Publishers, Inc., Carol Stream, Illinois 60188. All rights reserved.

Literary development and design: Koechel Peterson & Associates, Inc., Minneapolis, MN.

FaithWords
Hachette Book Group
237 Park Avenue New York, NY 10017
www.faithwords.com

Printed in the United States of America

First Edition: October 2013

10 9 8 7 6 5 4 3 2 1

FaithWords is a division of Hachette Book Group, Inc. The FaithWords name and logo are trademarks of Hachette Book Group, Inc.

The Hachette Speakers Bureau provides a wide range of authors for speaking events. To find out more, go to www.hachettespeakersbureau.com or call (866) 376-6591.

The publisher is not responsible for websites (or their content) that are not owned by the publisher.

Library of Congress Control Number: 2013946049

ISBN: 978-1-4555-5522-2

INTRODUCTION

Words have incredible power. Whenever we speak
something either good or bad, we give life to what
we are saying. Unfortunately, too many people
say negative things about themselves, about their
families, and about their futures.

Here is the key; you've got to send your words out in
the direction you want your life to go. You cannot
talk defeat and expect to have victory. You can't talk
lack and expect to have abundance. You will produce
what you say. If you want to know what you will be like
five years from now, just listen to what you are saying
about yourself. With our words we can either bless
our futures or we can curse our futures.

That's exactly where the personal application guide
you hold in your hand comes into play. In my book
I Declare, I revealed 31 declarations that can bring
God's favor and blessing to your life in a greater way.
Now, I have put together this companion guide that
will help insure that what you say about yourself and
others is positive, inspiring, and encouraging—a life
of consistent blessing one day at a time!

I'd love to have the privilege of walking you through the 31 "I Declares." In using this practical tool, you will find yourself daily challenged by insightful reflection questions, motivated by a specific call to action, and inspired by a relevant Scripture verse. Psychologically speaking, 31 days is time enough to have developed a new habit that I pray you will never give up, and by the time the days are complete, have also practiced and proven yourself victorious.

Each day in this personal application guide corresponds to a chapter in the original book. And each day in this guide contains four parts: the "I Declare" declaration, a reflection question, a personal application question, and a "My Day" Scripture page. The reflection question will highlight the main point of the day while the personal application question will relate the material to your own life and circumstances. Since writing out your answers can reinforce your thoughts as well as what God is showing you, space is provided for you to put on paper the answer to each question.

If you are willing to put these 31 declarations into action, God has much to say to you through the pages of this guide. He'll speak to you if you'll let Him, but He'll also want you to speak truthfully with Him. Take this faithful companion in hand, and begin each of your next 31 days with the only One who has the power to bless your future.

Start expecting good things. Learn to speak these words of blessing over yourself, your children, your finances, your health, and your future on a regular basis. If you'll use your words to declare victory and not defeat, you'll see God do amazing things, and I believe you'll live the abundant, overcoming, faith-filled life that He has in store.

Your life can be transformed, but not if you keep putting change off until tomorrow. A day has to come when you're ready to say, "This is the day." How about starting it with Day 1?

I Declare God's incredible blessings over my life.

I will see an explosion of God's goodness, a sudden widespread increase. I will experience the surpassing greatness of God's favor. It will elevate me to a level higher than I ever dreamed of. Explosive blessings are coming my way. This is my declaration.

Reflecting
on My Declaration

What does experiencing the surpassing greatness
of God's favor mean to you?

....

....

....

....

....

....

....

....

....

....

Seeing My Declaration in Action

God is saying, "You need to get ready.
Where you are is not permanent.
I have explosive blessings coming your way.
I will suddenly change things in your life."

What explosive blessings are you believing God for?

....

....

....

....

....

....

....

My Day 1 Scripture

*. . . the immeasurable (limitless, surpassing)
riches of His free grace (His unmerited favor) in
[His] kindness and goodness of heart toward us in Christ Jesus.*

EPHESIANS 2:7 AMP

I Declare I will experience God's faithfulness.

I will not worry. I will not doubt.
I will keep my trust in Him,
knowing that He will not fail me.
I will give birth to every promise
God put in my heart and I will
become everything God created
me to be. This is my declaration.

Reflecting
on My Declaration

God's faithfulness says a lot about His character. What results can we expect in our lives because we can trust God?

....

....

....

....

....

....

Seeing My Declaration in Action

God is saying, "Dare to trust Me. Quit being worried, stressed out, wondering if it will happen. I have you in the palm of My hand. I have never once failed before, and I'm not about to start now."

What promises has God spoken to your spirit? What dreams of your heart are you believing Him to bring to pass?

....

....

....

....

....

....

·····················○·····················

"Never will I leave you; never will I forsake you."
So we say with confidence, "The Lord is my helper;
I will not be afraid. What can mere mortals do to me?"

HEBREWS 13:5—6

I Declare I have the grace I need for today.

I am full of power, strength, and determination. Nothing I face will be too much for me. I will overcome every obstacle, outlast every challenge, and come through every difficulty better off than I was before. This is my declaration.

Reflecting
on My Declaration

What have you faced in the past that seemed to be too much for you? Were you able to use God's grace at that time to overcome that obstacle? If not, why do you think that was the case?

....

....

....

....

....

....

....

Seeing My Declaration in Action

God is saying, "My grace is there to help you through the dark valleys and still keep your head held high and your heart filled with love. I will give you the strength, the favor, the wisdom, the forgiveness to do what you need to do."

Every new day God has a fresh supply of grace. What obstacle are you facing today that you need God's immeasurable riches to overcome?

....

....

....

....

....

But he said to me, "My grace is sufficient for you, for my power is made perfect in weakness."

2 CORINTHIANS 12:9

I Declare it is not too late to accomplish everything God has placed in my heart.

I have not missed my window of opportunity. God has moments of favor in my future. He is preparing me right now because He is about to release a special grace to help me accomplish that dream. This is my time. This is my moment. I receive it today! This is my declaration.

Reflecting
on My Declaration

Are there areas of your life that you have put off
what you know God wants you to do? Perhaps a dream
or a goal? Why? What is holding you back?

....

....

....

....

....

....

....

....

....

Seeing My Declaration in Action

God is saying, "It's not too late to get started. You can still become everything I created you to be. But you must rise up in faith and passionately pursue what I have put in your heart."

What steps of faith will you take to accomplish what God has placed on your heart?

....

....

....

....

....

....

....

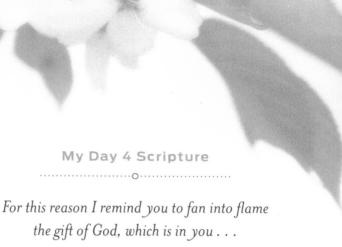

*For this reason I remind you to fan into flame
the gift of God, which is in you . . .*

2 TIMOTHY 1:6

I Declare I am grateful for who God is in my life and for what He's done.

I will not take for granted the people, the opportunities, and the favor He has blessed me with. I will look at what is right and not what is wrong. I will thank Him for what I have and not complain about what I don't have. I will see each day as a gift from God. My heart will overflow with praise and gratitude for all of His goodness. This is my declaration.

Reflecting
on My Declaration

This day is God's gift to you. What does
that mean to you? What difference will
it make to how you live this day?

Seeing My
Declaration in Action

God is saying, "This is the day I have made.
Rejoice and be glad in it! Don't take a minute for granted.
Live every day to the fullest . . . as though it could be your last."

If you only had an hour to live, who would you call?
What would you say? And what are you waiting for?

My Day 5 Scripture

Teach us to number our days,
that we may gain a heart of wisdom.

PSALM 90:12

I Declare a legacy of faith over my life.

I declare that I will store up blessings for future generations. My life is marked by excellence and integrity. Because I'm making right choices and taking steps of faith, others will want to follow me. God's abundance is surrounding my life today. This is my declaration.

Reflecting
on My Declaration

When you hear the phrase *a legacy of faith*,
what do you think of? What do you want to leave
behind that will affect generations to come?

Seeing My
Declaration in Action

*God is saying, "Every time you resist temptation,
are kind and respectful, and serve and give, you are storing
up mercy for someone in your family."*

How can you so live as to plant seeds of
faith that will help others to win?

....

....

....

....

....

....

....

My Day 6 Scripture

I am reminded of your sincere faith,
which first lived in your grandmother
Lois and in your mother Eunice and, I am
persuaded, now lives in you also.

2 TIMOTHY 1:5

I *Declare* that God has a great plan for my life.

He is directing my steps. And even though I may not always understand how, I know my situation is not a surprise to God. He will work out every detail to my advantage. In His perfect timing, everything will turn out right. This is my declaration.

Reflecting
on My Declaration

What have you experienced that you can't understand as to how it fits into God's plan for your life? Were you able to keep pressing forward? If not, how do you get unstuck?

....

....

....

....

....

....

....

....

....

Seeing My
Declaration in Action

God is saying, "I have the right pieces to make your life puzzle fit together. It may not make sense right now, but don't be discouraged—there's another piece coming that will pull it all together."

Setbacks, losses, disappointments—
what are you facing today that you need
to stay in faith regarding?

....

....

....

....

....

....

....

My Day 7 Scripture

·······················○·······················

"For I know the plans I have for you," declares the LORD, *"plans to prosper you and not to harm you, plans to give you hope and a future."*

JEREMIAH 29:11

I Declare God's dream for my life is coming to pass.

It will not be stopped by people, disappointments, or adversities. God has solutions to every problem I will ever face already lined up. The right people and the right breaks are in my future. I will fulfill my destiny. This is my declaration.

Reflecting
on My Declaration

What does it mean to you that God knows
exactly what you need—today and forever—
and is already taking care of you?

....

....

....

....

....

....

....

....

....

Seeing My Declaration in Action

God is saying, "I am in complete control. I know the end from the beginning. I know how to make it all work out. So live your life in peace."

What situation do you need to commit into God's hands and leave for Him to work out the solution?

....

....

....

....

....

....

....

·······················○·······················

"Remember the former things, those of long ago;
I am God, and there is no other;
I am God, and there is none like me.
I make known the end from the beginning,
from ancient times, what is still to come.
I say, 'My purpose will stand,
and I will do all that I please.'"

ISAIAH 46:9—10

I Declare

unexpected blessings are coming my way.

I will move forward from barely making it to having more than enough. God will open up supernatural doors for me. He will speak to the right people about me. I will see Ephesians 3:20, exceedingly, abundantly, above-and-beyond favor and increase in my life. This is my declaration.

Reflecting
on My Declaration

To live in the favor of God—can you
describe what that looks like? How might
God bring opportunities across your path
that are greater than you can imagine?

....

....

....

....

....

....

....

....

....

Seeing My
Declaration in Action

God is saying, "I have amazing things in your future.
I have doors that will open wider than you thought possible.
If you have been faithful, your payday is on its way."

When you are faithful in the little things,
God will give you greater things. What are the
"little things" that you need to be faithful in today?

....

....

....

....

....

....

·························○·························

*Now to him who is able to do immeasurably
more than all we ask or imagine, according to his
power that is at work within us, to him be glory
in the church and in Christ Jesus throughout all
generations, for ever and ever! Amen.*

EPHESIANS 3:20—21

I Declare that God will accelerate His plan for my life as I put my trust in Him.

I will accomplish my dreams faster than I thought possible. It will not take years to overcome an obstacle, to get out of debt, or to meet the right person. God is doing things faster than before. He will give me victory sooner than I think. He has blessings that will thrust me years ahead. This is my declaration.

Reflecting
on My Declaration

In His first public miracle, Jesus produced
the finest-quality wine in a moment in time.
What does that story tell you about what He
can accomplish in your life?

....

....

....

....

....

....

....

....

Seeing My Declaration in Action

God is saying, "I can turn your water into wine. I can do in a split second what might otherwise take you many years. Just do what I ask, and I will bring it to pass."

God is in the accelerating business.
What acceleration are you believing
God will do in your life?

·····················○·····················

*His mother said to the servants,
"Do whatever he tells you. . . ."
They did so, and the master of the
banquet tasted the water that had
been turned into wine.*

JOHN 2:5—9

I Declare Ephesians 3:20 over my life.

God will do exceedingly, abundantly above all that I ask or think. Because I honor Him, His blessings will chase me down and overtake me. I will be in the right place at the right time. People will go out of their way to be good to me. I am surrounded by God's favor. This is my declaration.

Reflecting
on My Declaration

In what ways have you experienced the
blessings of God in the past? Can you
explain why His favor is upon you?

....

....

....

....

....

....

....

....

....

Seeing My
Declaration in Action

God is saying, "You need to prepare for an exceeding, abundant, above-and-beyond life. My high favor abides on those who walk with Me in faith."

Blessings overtake us when we obey God's voice. What is He calling you to obey today?

....

....

....

....

....

....

....

·························○·························

And all these blessings shall come upon
you and overtake you if you heed the
voice of the Lord your God.

DEUTERONOMY 28:2 AMP

I Declare I am special and extraordinary.

I am not average! I have been custom-made. I am one of a kind. Of all the things God created, what He is the most proud of is me. I am His masterpiece, His most prized possession. I will keep my head held high, knowing I am a child of the most high God, made in His very image. This is my declaration.

Reflecting
on My Declaration

What do you believe that God really thinks about you?
Do you believe you bring Him joy?

....

....

....

....

....

....

....

....

Seeing My Declaration in Action

God is saying, "You're amazing. You're beautiful. You're created in My image. You are My masterpiece. You are My child!"

In what ways do you need to learn to receive your value from your Heavenly Father rather than from other people?

....

....

....

....

....

....

....

For we are God's masterpiece. He has created us anew in Christ Jesus, so we can do the good things he planned for us long ago.

EPHESIANS 2:10 NLT

I Declare that God is bringing about new seasons of growth.

I will not get stagnant and hold on to the old. I will be open to change, knowing that God has something better in front of me. New doors of opportunity, new relationships, and new levels of favor are in my future. This is my declaration.

Reflecting
on My Declaration

How has God used situations to stretch you and to hopefully push you into new dimensions? Did you embrace the change? If not, what was the result?

....

....

....

....

....

....

....

....

Seeing My
Declaration in Action

God is saying, "Don't fight change. I wouldn't allow it if I didn't have a purpose in it. Embrace it, and you will step into the fullness of what I have in store."

God loves you too much to just leave you alone. How can you embrace the changes He is trying to work in your life right now?

....

....

....

....

....

....

·······················○·······················

Woe to him who strives with his Maker! . . . Shall the clay say to him who fashions it, What do you think you are making? or, Your work has no handles?

ISAIAH 45:9 AMP

I Declare that I will use my words to bless people.

I will speak favor and victory over my family, friends, and loved ones. I will help call out their seeds of greatness by telling them "I'm proud of you, I love you, you are amazing, you are talented, you are beautiful, you will do great things in life." This is my declaration.

Reflecting
on My Declaration

Can you recall times when your words had a
positive impact on someone's life? What did you
say, and why did it become a blessing?

....

....

....

....

....

....

....

....

Seeing My
Declaration in Action

*God is saying, "Your words have the power to bless others
in ways you could never dream. When you speak blessings,
you release My favor into lives in a greater way."*

How will you use your words to release God's
supernatural power into as many people
as possible today?

My Day 14 Scripture

......................○......................

The tongue has the power of life and death,
and those who love it will eat its fruit.

PROVERBS 18:21

I Declare that I have a sound mind filled with good thoughts, not thoughts of defeat.

By faith, I am well able. I am anointed. I am equipped. I am empowered. My thoughts are guided by God's word every day. No obstacle can defeat me, because my mind is programmed for victory. This is my declaration.

Reflecting
on My Declaration

God says He has crowned you with favor. Do you agree
with Him? Really? Do you live accordingly?

. . . .

. . . .

. . . .

. . . .

. . . .

. . . .

. . . .

. . . .

. . . .

Seeing My Declaration in Action

*God is saying, "I have already crowned you with favor. I am ready
to release the promises that have your name on them. By faith,
declare that it is true and walk and talk like you are blessed."*

What areas of your thinking require reprogramming to
believe you already have God's blessing? In what ways
will you put actions behind your faith?

....

....

....

....

....

....

My Day 15 Scripture

*Surely, L*ORD*, you bless the righteous;*
you surround them with your favor as with a shield.

PSALM 5:12

I *Declare* that I will live as a healer.

I am sensitive to the needs of those around me. I will lift the fallen, restore the broken, and encourage the discouraged. I am full of compassion and kindness. I won't just look for a miracle; I will become someone's miracle by showing God's love and mercy everywhere I go. This is my declaration.

Reflecting
on My Declaration

When it comes to helping hurting people, are you more like the Good Samaritan, who helped bring restoration, or the priest, who passed on by? To what degree do you "love your neighbor as yourself"?

Seeing My
Declaration in Action

God is saying, "I want you to become like Me. Be a healer, a restorer, one who takes the time to wipe away others' tears. Your job is not to judge but to be full of encouragement and mercy."

What steps will you take to come alongside someone who is hurting and become their miracle?

........................o........................

Brothers and sisters, if someone is caught in a sin, you who live by the Spirit should restore that person gently. But watch yourselves, or you also may be tempted. Carry each other's burdens, and in this way you will fulfill the law of Christ.

GALATIANS 6:1—2

I *Declare* I will put actions behind my faith.

I will not be passive or indifferent. I will demonstrate my faith by taking bold steps to move toward what God has put in my heart. My faith will not be hidden; it will be seen. I know when God sees my faith He will show up and do amazing things. This is my declaration.

Reflecting
on My Declaration

How would you describe your faith? Do you have the "never say die" attitude that the paralyzed man had? Do you dare to take action that God sees?

Seeing My Declaration in Action

God is saying, "I want you to have a faith I can see and not just hear. I want you to demonstrate your faith by putting actions behind what you believe."

What are you believing God for that you need to put action behind in a demonstration of your faith?

....

....

....

....

....

....

....

My Day 17 Scripture

························○························

When Jesus saw their faith, he said to the paralyzed man,
"Son, your sins are forgiven."

MARK 2:5

I Declare

breakthroughs are coming in my life, sudden bursts of God's goodness.

Not a trickle. Not a stream. But a flood of God's power. A flood of healing. A flood of wisdom. A flood of favor. I am a breakthrough person, and I choose to live breakthrough minded. I am expecting God to overwhelm me with His goodness and amaze me with His favor. This is my declaration.

Reflecting
on My Declaration

When you think of God's goodness toward you,
what comes to mind? Do you think "trickle,"
"stream," or "flood"?

....

....

....

....

....

....

....

....

Seeing My Declaration in Action

God is saying, "Enlarge your vision. Dare to stretch your faith. I want to release My favor and increase like a flood and overwhelm you with My goodness."

What is keeping the God of the breakthrough from releasing a flood of His power in your life that nothing can stop?

·······················○·······················

[David] said, "As waters break out, God has broken out against my enemies by my hand."

1 CHRONICLES 14:11

I Declare there is an anointing of ease on my life.

God is going before me making crooked places straight. His yoke is easy and His burden is light. I will not continually struggle. What used to be difficult will not be difficult anymore. God's favor and blessing on my life is lightening the load and taking the pressure off. This is my declaration.

Reflecting
on My Declaration

God wants to make your life easier. Do you believe
that, or do you think He wants to make you struggle?
Do you see Him anointing your head with oil?

Seeing My Declaration in Action

God is saying, "I am on the throne, and I am directing every one of your steps. There are good breaks just ahead for you. Surely My goodness and mercy will follow you wherever you go."

What solutions to your problems are you believing God has already lined up?

....

....

....

....

....

....

....

............................O............................

"Take my yoke upon you and learn from me, for I am gentle and humble in heart, and you will find rest for your souls. For my yoke is easy and my burden is light."

MATTHEW 11:29—30

I Declare that I am calm and peaceful.

I will not let people or circumstances upset me. I will rise above every difficulty, knowing that God has given me the power to remain calm. I choose to live my life happy, bloom where I am planted, and let God fight my battles. This is my declaration.

Reflecting
on My Declaration

When you allow what someone says or does to upset
you, you allow them to control you. Is this a recurrent
problem in your life? If so, why?

....

....

....

....

....

....

....

....

....

Seeing My
Declaration in Action

God is saying, "You can't control what others say or do to you, but you have the right to not get offended or angry. Your worth lies in Me alone."

What are the hot buttons in your life that others push that you have a right to ignore and change?

....

....

....

....

....

....

....

....

......................○......................

Do not be anxious about anything, but in every situation, by prayer and petition, with thanksgiving, present your requests to God. And the peace of God, which transcends all understanding, will guard your hearts and your minds in Christ Jesus.

PHILIPPIANS 4:6—7

I Declare God's supernatural favor over my life.

What I could not make happen on my own, God will make happen for me. Supernatural opportunities, healing, restoration, and breakthroughs are coming my way. I am getting stronger, healthier, and wiser. I will discover talent that I didn't know I had, and I will accomplish my God-given dream. This is my declaration.

Reflecting
on My Declaration

That secret dream in your heart—do you
believe God put it there . . . or that He
wants to bring it to pass? How so?

. . . .

. . . .

. . . .

. . . .

. . . .

. . . .

. . . .

. . . .

Seeing My Declaration in Action

*God is saying, "Is there anything too hard for Me?
I am all-powerful. I can turn any situation around.
I can bring your dreams and your secret desires to
pass. I will amaze you with My goodness."*

**What supernatural increase are you
believing God for?**

....

....

....

....

....

....

My Day 21 Scripture

··O··

And God is able to bless you abundantly, so that
in all things at all times, having all that you need,
you will abound in every good work.

2 CORINTHIANS 9:8

I Declare I will live victoriously.

*I was created in the image of God.
I have the DNA of a winner. I am
wearing a crown of favor. Royal blood
flows through my veins. I am the head,
never the tail, above never beneath.
I will live with purpose, passion, and
praise, knowing that I was destined to
live in victory. This is my declaration.*

Reflecting
on My Declaration

God sees you as a king or a queen with
royalty in your blood. How do you see yourself?
Are you living up to your royal privileges?

....

....

....

....

....

....

....

....

....

Seeing My Declaration in Action

*God is saying, "As long as you are alive, it is your
time to reign in power through My Son Jesus. Walk
like a king, talk like a king, think like a king. Don't
go by what you see. Go by what you know."*

What strongholds will you break that are
keeping you back from stepping up to
become who God created you to be?

....

....

....

....

....

....

....

·······················○·······················

For if, by the trespass of the one man, death reigned through that one man, how much more will those who receive God's abundant provision of grace and of the gift of righteousness reign in life through the one man, Jesus Christ!

ROMANS 5:17

I Declare I am a people builder.

*I will look for opportunities to encourage others
to bring out the best in them and to help them
accomplish their dreams. I will speak words of
faith and victory, affirming them, approving
them, letting them know they are valued. I will
call out their seeds of greatness, helping them
to rise higher and become all that God created
them to be. This is my declaration.*

Reflecting
on My Declaration

Everyone needs to be valued and appreciated.
What kinds of seeds are you planting in loved
ones and friends? Do they know you love them
and how proud you are of them?

....

....

....

....

....

....

....

....

....

Seeing My
Declaration in Action

God is saying, "You do not realize the power you hold to bless others. Plant seeds of encouragement, celebrate others' successes, pray when they struggle, and always urge them on."

What will you do today to let someone know that you are their number one fan?

....

....

....

....

....

....

....

My Day 23 Scripture

·······················○·······················

Your love has given me great joy and encouragement, because you, brother, have refreshed the hearts of the Lord's people.

PHILEMON 1:7

I Declare I will speak only positive words of faith and victory over myself, my family, and my future.

I will not use my words to describe the situation. I will use my words to change my situation. I will call in favor, good breaks, healing, and restoration. I will not talk to God about how big my problems are. I will talk to my problems about how big my God is. This is my declaration.

Reflecting
on My Declaration

If your words were replayed at the end of the day,
what would you hear? What do you speak about
yourself, your family, and your future?

Seeing My
Declaration in Action

*God is saying, "Pay attention to the words you speak.
Don't talk about the way you are. Talk about the way you
want to be. Speak victory over your life always."*

What are some specific ways you can change the
way you talk and move from defeat to victory?

. . . .

. . . .

. . . .

. . . .

. . . .

. . . .

. . . .

My Day 24 Scripture

......................○........................

*"Truly I tell you, if anyone says to this mountain,
'Go, throw yourself into the sea,' and does not doubt
in their heart but believes that what they say will
happen, it will be done for them. Therefore I tell
you, whatever you ask for in prayer, believe that
you have received it, and it will be yours."*

MARK 11:23—24

I Declare I will not just survive; I will thrive!

I will prosper despite every difficulty that may come my way. I know every setback is a setup for a comeback. I will not get stagnant, give up on my dreams, or settle where I am. I know one touch of God's favor can change everything. I'm ready for a year of blessings and a year of thriving! This is my declaration.

Reflecting
on My Declaration

Would you describe yourself as one who is surviving or
thriving, holding on and maintaining or increasing?
How does God factor into your thinking?

....

....

....

....

....

....

....

....

Seeing My Declaration in Action

God is saying, "I have new seasons in front of you. I have new doors I want to open. I want the next part of your life to be better than the first part."

God took the fives loaves and two fish and multiplied it to feed thousands. What ways are you expecting God to increase you in a greater way?

....

....

....

....

....

....

....

But while Joseph was there in the prison, the LORD was with him; he showed him kindness and granted him favor in the eyes of the prison warden. So the warden put Joseph in charge . . . and he was made responsible for all that was done there. . . . because the LORD was with Joseph and gave him success in whatever he did.

GENESIS 39:20—23

I Declare I will choose faith over fear!

I will meditate on what is positive and what is good about my situation. I will use my energy not to worry but to believe. Fear has no part in my life. I will not dwell on negative, discouraging thoughts. My mind is set on what God says about me. I know His plan for me is for success, victory, and abundance. This is my declaration.

Reflecting
on My Declaration

What are the fears and anxieties that play over and over again in your mind? Have they taken root?

....

....

....

....

....

....

....

....

....

....

Seeing My Declaration in Action

God is saying, "Place your life in My hands. I will supply all of your needs. I will guide and direct your steps to victory and success. Always choose faith over fear."

What statements of faith will you use to combat and defeat the fears that trouble you?

....

....

....

....

....

....

....

....

. . . *for everyone born of God overcomes the world. This is the victory that has overcome the world, even our faith. Who is it that overcomes the world? Only the one who believes that Jesus is the Son of God.*

1 JOHN 5:4—5

I Declare I am equipped for every good work God has planned for me.

I am anointed and empowered by the Creator of the universe. Every bondage, every limitation, is being broken off of me. This is my time to shine. I will rise higher, overcome every obstacle, and experience victory like never before! This is my declaration.

Reflecting
on My Declaration

When you face tough times, what do you tell yourself
about your situation? How does your faith impact how
you make it through difficulties?

....

....

....

....

....

....

....

....

Seeing My Declaration in Action

God is saying, "You don't have to struggle and try to make things happen. It's already in you: the strength, the creativity, the ideas. Walk in My anointing. My blessings and grace are yours."

What promises has God given in His Word to equip and empower you with everything you need to walk in joy and strength?

....

....

....

....

....

....

·······················○·······················

*But you have an anointing from the Holy One,
and all of you know the truth.*

1 JOHN 2:20

I Declare that I will ask God for big things in my life.

I will pray bold prayers and expect big and believe big. I will ask God to bring to pass those hidden dreams that are deep in my heart. If certain promises don't look like they will happen, I will not be intimidated and give up. I will pray with boldness, expecting God to show Himself strong, knowing that nothing is too difficult for Him. This is my declaration.

Reflecting
on My Declaration

How do you categorize your prayers—as little
or big? What does that say about what you
believe about God's character?

....

....

....

....

....

....

....

....

....

....

Seeing My Declaration in Action

God is saying, "Ask Me for big things. Ask Me for those hidden dreams that I've planted in your heart. Ask Me for those unborn promises that may seem unlikely to happen in the natural."

Dare to ask God for your greatest dreams, your greatest desires. What are you asking from Him?

....

....

....

....

....

....

....

....

·······················O·······················

Ask me, and I will make the nations your inheritance,
the ends of the earth your possession.

PSALM 2:8

I Declare God is working all things together for my good.

He has a master plan for my life. There may be things I don't understand right now, but I'm not worried. I know all the pieces aren't here yet. One day it will all come together and everything will make sense. I will see God's amazing plan taking me places I never dreamed of. This is my declaration.

Reflecting
on My Declaration

How do you respond to those situations in life that
cause you to ask, "Why did this happen to me?"
Is God in your big picture view?

Seeing My
Declaration in Action

God is saying, "I have a great plan for your life.
Nothing that comes into your life catches Me by surprise.
I will work it to your advantage and good."

Whether it's in the area of your finances, your
career, or your marriage, where do you need to start
exercising a deep inner trust in God?

....

....

....

....

....

....

....

·························○·························

*And we know that in all things God works
for the good of those who love him, who have
been called according to his purpose.*

ROMANS 8:28

I Declare God is going before me making crooked places straight.

He has already lined up the right people, the right opportunities and solutions to problems I haven't had. No person, no sickness, no disappointment, can stop His plan. What He promised will come to pass. This is my declaration.

Reflecting
on My Declaration

If you believe that God is going out before you, how should that influence your prayers and confidence? Is it making that impact on yours?

....

....

....

....

....

....

....

....

....

Seeing My Declaration in Action

God is saying, "You may be facing a situation that seems impossible, but I hold your future in My hands. I will go before you and fight your battles and make a way for you."

It's not by your own strength or power. What life battles and challenges are you believing God to win for you?

....

....

....

....

....

....

....

My Day 30 Scripture

·····················○·····················

Hear, Israel: You are now about to cross the Jordan to go in and dispossess nations greater and stronger than you, with large cities that have walls up to the sky. . . . But be assured today that the LORD your God is the one who goes across ahead of you like a devouring fire. He will destroy them; he will subdue them before you.

DEUTERONOMY 9:1—3

I Declare everything that doesn't line up with God's vision for my life is subject to change.

Sickness, trouble, lack, mediocrity, are not permanent. They are only temporary. I will not be moved by what I see but by what I know. I am a victor and never a victim. I will become all God has created me to be. This is my declaration.

Reflecting
on My Declaration

Joseph had a big dream in his heart that helped him
overcome huge difficulties. What is your dream?

....

....

....

....

....

....

....

....

....

....

Seeing My Declaration in Action

God is saying, "Do not allow discouragement to cloud your vision. If what you see does not match up with the vision I put in your heart, it is just another stop on the way to your destiny."

How will you use the vision God has put in your heart to make it through to your destiny?

....

....

....

....

....

....

....

My Day 31 Scripture

........................o........................

But Joseph said to them, "Don't be afraid.
Am I in the place of God? You intended to harm
me, but God intended it for good to accomplish
what is now being done, the saving of many lives."

GENESIS 50:19—20

For Further Application

I believe that as a result of the truths God has revealed to you and the faith actions you have taken through this guide, things in the spiritual realm have been set into motion in your life. Curses have been broken and blessings are on their way. Realize, however, that this is only the beginning. There will never be a time in your life when you will not face mountains of challenges and difficulties that require you to make declarations of God's favor and victory.

When you declare not in your authority but in the authority of the Son of the Living God, all the forces of heaven come to attention. The mighty armies of the unseen Most High God will stand behind you. Let me tell you, no power can stand against our God. No sickness. No addiction. No fear. No legal trouble. When you speak and you do not doubt, the mountains of discouragement and closed doors will be removed.

Nothing can keep you from God's best in your career, your relationships, or your health.

Remember, your mountains will respond to your voice. There's nothing more powerful than you declaring victory over your life. Here are some of the declarations you need to memorize and always have ready for life's battles:

- "I declare I walk in the blessing of almighty God. I am filled with wisdom. I make good choices. I have clear direction."

- "I declare I am blessed with creativity, with good ideas, with courage, with strength, with ability."

- "I declare I am blessed with good health, a good family, good friends, and a long life."

- "I declare I am blessed with promotion, with success, with an obedient heart, and with a positive outlook."

❧ "I declare whatever I put my hands to will prosper and succeed. I will be blessed in the city and blessed in the field. I will be blessed when I go in and when I go out."

❧ "I declare I will lend and not borrow, and I will be above and not beneath."

❧ "I declare right now that every negative word, every curse that has ever been spoken over me, is broken in the name of Jesus."

❧ "I declare the negative things that have been in my family even for generations will no longer have any effect on me."

❧ "I declare that from this day forward I will experience a new sense of freedom, a new happiness, and a new fulfillment."

❧ "I declare I am blessed!"

STAY**CONNECTED,**
BE**BLESSED.**

From thoughtful articles to powerful blogs,
podcasts and more, JoelOsteen.com is full of
inspirations that will give you encouragement and
confidence in your daily life.

AVAILABLE ON JOELOSTEEN.COM

today's W**O**RD

This daily devotional from Joel
and Victoria will help you grow
in your relationship with the Lord
and equip you to be everything
God intends you to be.

**Plus, connect with us
on your favorite sites.**

Joel Osteen
STREAMING

Miss a broadcast? Watch Joel
Osteen on demand, and see
Joel LIVE on Sundays.

Joel Osteen
PODCAST

Put Joel in your pocket!
The podcast is a great way
to listen to Joel where you
want, when you want.

facebook.com/JoelOsteen

twitter.com/JoelOsteen

Thanks for helping us make a difference in
the lives of millions around the world.

Notes

Notes

Notes

Notes

Notes